A CURLEW'S CRY

by

MICHAEL TOD

By the same Author

The Silver Tide
The Second Wave
The Golden Flight
Now available in a single volume -
The Dorset Squirrels
Dolphinsong

ISBN 1 898225 01 X

4th Edition 2003

Designed by Barbara Anne Knight

Published by Cadno Books,
PO Box 34, Abergavenny, NP8 1YN.

Printed in Wales by
Dinefwr Press,
Rawlings Road, Llandybie,
Carmarthenshire, SA18 3YD.

A CURLEW'S CRY

by

MICHAEL TOD

In a poet's wood
All the trees are of crystal
He can hide nowhere.

Lim Do Tchae

This book is dedicated to my late aunt,
Georgina Hoare.

'A harbour light seen from a stormy sea.'

Index of poems and first lines

ABACUS OF GOD (THE) 33
A Bushman stood on the gleaming sand 43
A CURLEW'S CRY 1
ADAM AND EVE IN ORBIT 20
A DROP OF DOGGEREL 12
A FLY IN AMBER 27
A mountain stands behind Y Fenni town 1
AN END TO ALL THIS (From BOYHOOD) 6
A NEST OF HORNETS 16
A night in Africa 24
A NIGHT LONG REMEMBERED 32
A PARADOX 30
APPRENTICE (From BOYHOOD) 5
ARMISTICE DAY AT ELY CATHEDRAL 1957 18
At sixteen years I was apprentice bound 5
BASHER B. 36
Below the Darren where the ravens nest 28
BLESS THIS HOUSE 22
BOYHOOD 2
BUSHMAN'S TALE (THE) 24
But it was Scouting that I loved the best 4
BUTTERFLY (HOBSON'S) 12
CASTELL CADNO 41
CHESIL BEACH 45
CHURCH BY THE LAKE (THE) 33
CULTURE UNFATHOMED 14
CURLEW'S CRY (A) 1
CWM CADNO DAYS (From BOYHOOD) 3
Do you remember Uncle Taffy? 13
DROP OF DOGGEREL (A) 12
Dusk in mid-afternoon 22
FAIR ISLE'S SONG 39
FEELING WELSH 35
Five, four, three, two, one. 20
FLY IN AMBER (A) 27
Frogs (ONE GOOD CHURN) 9

From Lulworth Cove to Kimmeridge 30
FROM WHENCE COMETH 15
GLORIA 7
Gloria's Transit van was her pride and joy 7
HANDS UP FOR A THIRD MILLENNIUM 26
HAREBELLS 8
Hearing a distant curlew's bubbling cry 1
Helen, when first I saw 10
HOBSON'S BUTTERFLY 12
HORNETS (A NEST OF) 16
HUMAN CANNONBALL (THE) 31
I, Fair Isle, call to Thinking Men 39
I interviewed a man last night 12
I know you'd like to hear about the girls 6
I'm Joseph - just a carpenter 46
In chapel as a child 8
I need the sight of hills 15
I stood upon the mighty Chesil Bank 33
I was just ten years old 35
JANE'S PLATE 28
JOSEPH'S CHILD 46
KISSING HANDS 10
LARKS AND OWLS 9
MY BROTHER TIM 40
My brother Tim makes poetry 40
MY DAFFODIL 17
My garden had a Russian Privet hedge 17
MY HEDGE 17
MY HILL 11
NEST OF HORNETS (A) 16
NIGHT LONG REMEMBERED (A) 32
NOT ALWAYS BLACK 31
NOW - AND THEN 47
Now, When you see a squirrel on a branch 47
ONE GOOD CHURN 19
One long past Spring I walked alone 19
OUR SUGAR LOAF 1
One summer we had hornets at the farm 16
Only the whales and dolphins have evolved 26
PAPER BOY (THE) 30
PARADOX (A) 30
Pity the Paper Boy in Winter 30

PLAIN JANE 1
PONDERING THE INFINITE 21
RHYTHMS OF THE SEA (From BOYHOOD) 2
ROCKALL'S SONG 38
SCOUTING (From BOYHOOD) 4
SECRET OF THE UNIVERSE (THE) 43
Some men and women 9
SUGAR LOAF (OUR) 1
TAFFY'S PLAN 13
Ten million years ago a fly 27
Ten years ago, deep in the hills 41
THE ABACUS OF GOD 33
THE BUSHMAN'S TALE 24
THE CHURCH BY THE LAKE 33
THE HUMAN CANNONBALL 31
The Mount of Olives 32
THE THOUGHTS OF SOME 10
The thoughts of some are sparkling 10
THE SECRET OF THE UNIVERSE 43
The wind of Spring was singing 33
They call us black. Perhaps we seem that way 31
They have no culture, they are savages 14
The young men called her plain 1
They're going to build a wind-farm 11
THOUGHTS OF SOME (THE) 10
Time always was and Time will always be 21
Today there is no wind 45
Two caterpillars chomped along a leaf 12
Two frogs fell in a bowl of cream 9
We stood a hundred Servicemen and girls 18
We were a rotten class 36
When Granville's Splendid Circus came to town 31
When I was born the sunlit sparkling sea 2, 38
When I was ten we left that magic coast 3

A CURLEW'S CRY

Hearing a distant curlew's bubbling cry
My heart with hiraeth fills.
This sad, lonely sound distils
Sun and wind on Wales' hills.

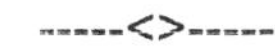

OUR SUGAR LOAF

A mountain stands behind Y Fenni town,
Not grand as mountains go, but very dear
To those who watch it change, white, green then brown,
To mark the passing seasons of the year.

We walk the beechwoods of Saint Mary's Vale,
The close-cropped grass above Llanwenarth Breast,
We stroll through stunted oaks, the Deri trail
Or take the Rholben ridge to reach the crest.

When pressures mount and life seems full of strain,
We climb this hill and breathe the sparkling air.
The peace and solitude there eases pain
And troubles shrink and often disappear.

If we must leave our lovely town to study, work or fight,
We know we're nearly home again when our Sugar Loaf's in sight.

PLAIN JANE

The young men called her plain and went their way.
"It's pretty girls we want," I heard them say,
But, once, I saw the love-light in her eyes,
And Jane, though plain, was beautiful that day.

When I was born the sunlit, sparkling sea
Patterned the ceiling, light delighting me,
And, as I grew, that sea was always near,
Gull-cries and wave sounds ever in my ear.
Barefoot amongst the worm-casts on the rippled sand
I wandered free, my little body tanned
By salty breezes that the grown-ups shun,
My child's eyes narrowed by a hazy sun
That warms the pools bait-diggers leave behind.
A seagull feather was a special find
Held high, vibrating, thrumming in my hand
Then thrown aloft to spin towards the land,
Forgotten in a moment; something new
Would catch my eye: a bright green copper screw,
Sand-polished glass, a cork, a piece of wood,
Cuttlefish bones or whelk's eggs, each was good
To handle, smell, abandon - half a minute's joy -
Each common thing a treasure to this little boy.

I learned the run of currents, times of tides,
I knew the sandbar where the flatfish hides,
I'd find the oyster-catchers' hidden nest
Amongst the flotsam. Their alarm made manifest
Through plaintive piping, tricks with broken wings
Decoying me away. But other things
Along the high tide mark would catch my eye,
A driftwood dragon, seaweed crisp and dry,
(My favourite was many-bubbled bladder-wrack,
Pinching each black balloon to make it crack)
Dead guillemots, striped Brasso tins
From Naval ships, dried dogfish with sandpaper skins
And soggy sailors-hats blown overboard.
Such riches - I'd collect a hoard
And leave them on the beach, run home for tea,
Tomorrow would bring more in from the sea.

Then there were boats - learning to row and sail -
My brother's voice: "Don't let the painter trail."
The skill of sculling with a single oar,
The thrill of landing on an unknown shore
Across the bay, to sleep beneath the sky,
Only a sail to keep the bedding dry. >>>

Rising at dawn to catch an off-shore breeze,
Watching for catspaws, grey on sunlit seas,
Feeling the ropes as stiff as rods, the canvas taut,
Heeling with gunwale dipping, braced against a thwart.
Then sudden calm, bow-wave and bubbling wake subside
To drift in silence on the morning tide.
Alert for eddies warning 'sunken rocks'
We'd drift along. We had no clocks,
The angle of the sun, the rate of flow,
Sounds from the land, the way the seabirds go,
Told us the hour. So were these early years to me
A life in tune with tides and subtle rhythms of the sea.

-----<>-----

BOYHOOD: Part Two: Cwm Cadno Days

When I was ten, we left that magic coast;
The lovely hills of Wales were to host
My adolescence. There upon a hillside farm
I grew to manhood. There I learned the charm
Of misty valleys seen from high above,
The croak of ravens, call of curlews, coo of dove.
To wake to mooing as the cows came in,
Rattle of buckets, bark of cowman's dog, the din
Of milking time, muted by distance, penetrating sleep.
Breakfast of porridge, pile into the Jeep
And down the hill, churns clanking on the back, to school
That was an alien place to be, I'd play the fool
And waste the time I spent there - that was me -
To be indoors was living purgatory.

I loved to shoot. I learned the marksman's skill
And many a rabbit shot, (though now I never kill)
I'd track the foxes' pawprints in the snow
To find a still-born lamb, eyes taken by a crow,
Then back to join the others on the sledge,
Fly down the meadow, crash into the hedge,
Shouting and laughing in the frost-still air;
The world was somewhere else - we had no care.
On summer evenings we would go to swim
Down to the Usk, then watch the swallows skim
The water, where migrating elvers swam. >>>

Sometimes in mountain streams we'd build a dam
With stones and turf and moss to make our pool
Then wallow naked in the water cool.
How innocent we were with simple joys,
All Wales for our playground, lucky boys!

-----<>-----

BOYHOOD: Part Three: Scouting

But it was Scouting that I loved the best.
Tracking and hiking, passing every test
To win my badges. Learn the woodsman's lore,
Tree-felling, cabin-building, use of axe and saw.
Master my knots, throw bridges over streams,
Climbing, canoeing, caving - many schemes
Of high adventure filled each holiday.
The Summer Camp, when we would go away
To Exmoor, Western Wales or Wareham Heath
Set up our tents and sleep beneath
A canvas roof. To wake to pigeons in the pines,
Crawl from warm beds to make bee-lines
Through grass and bracken to a smelly loo.
A trail of footprints in the morning dew.

Breakfast was eaten standing in the chill,
Before the sun had cleared the eastern hill.
Blue-rimmed enamel plates piled high with beans,
That staple base of many camp cuisines,
With smoky stews, burnt custard, soggy duff.
To hungry boys it all was good enough
For WE had cooked it, called it 'lovely grub'.
Wide games we played through wood and scrub,
Built gadgets out of sticks and string,
Devices that would hold just anything
And keep our campsite smart. Then after dark
We'd gather round a campfire; put a spark
To birchbark tinder, well dried logs. There, in the glow,
Our favourite songs we'd sing, with more gusto
Than melody. In sun or rain each joyful day would pass.
Fond memories now, mere shadows on the grass.

-----<>-----

At sixteen years I was apprentice-bound.
A job at Seargeant Brothers had been found,
To suit my aspirations to create
Beautiful things - bookbinding thought appropriate.
I learned to fold and sew the pages of a book
And worked with glue and paste, but never overlook
The need to keep the workbench clean, and free
From sticky splashes, lest the foreman see
And castigate this 'Mucky lad' - the boy
He had to train and teach that loving joy
A real craftsman had in all he did and made.

Leather was good to handle, every shade
Of colour held. Many a different skin,
Stiff vellum, glossy basil, skivers thin
I had to learn to work with. Cut with care,
Softened and folded, rubbed down on a pair
Of covers, spines then bound with cords
And clamped into a press between two boards.

I loved, and feared, the power guillotine,
Its heavy blade, honed razor keen,
Sheared stacks of paper with a single stroke.
For me, though safely guarded, how it would invoke
A fears of fingers lost. But big Old Bill
Who worked this dread machine, had still
All those he had been born with, but it was his joke
To keep two folded down and tell new folk
Joining the firm, how they had been chopped off
Elaborating blood and gore, then scoff
When they felt faint and moved away.
Bill loved this little joke, it made his day.

I also learned the way to form a gel
For marbling paper, boiling seaweed well,
Letting the extract set, and on the top,
In random patterns, colours drop.
Tradition specified red, blue and black,
Followed by ox-gall, pushing back
The colours, making marble veins.
Lay on the paper, taking pains >>>

To get no bubbles - when it was quite smooth
Lift by one corner, carefully remove
The paper, hang it on a line -
Each sheet unique, an individual design.

Sometimes I worked with leaves of gold
Beaten so thin that, if I lost my hold,
The leaf would float on air, as light
(Though made of metal) as a feather might.
The gold was melted with a heated tool
To block-print titles which, when cool,
Would not rub off, but glowed,
Impressed in leather, never to corrode.

On special books we used these leaves of gold
To gild the edge of pages. In a press we'd hold
The sheets clamped tight together, then, with white
Of egg, we'd paint the surface - lay the gold on right,
And burnish with an agate. Thus I learned my trade.
I wonder now: where are those books I made?

-----<>-----

BOYHOOD: Part Five: An End to All of This

I know you'd like to hear about the girls
I courted then, who, when and where. These pearls
Of memories are safe inside my private shell
And not for sharing. So I'll never tell
Of furtive fumblings, cuddles in the hay,
Walks by the river. I will not betray
The secret pleasures while we learned how we
Were different from one another, he from she!
School 'Social Evenings', playing Postman's Knock,
Shy kisses. Home by ten o'clock.

Dear Fanny Jones's vain attempt to teach
Me how to dance - she would beseech
Me, towering above, to move my feet
In time with something that she called 'the beat'
But I was deaf to. In the end
She gave up trying. She is still my friend.

Mr. Medina, living down below the farm
Befriended me. With his so easy charm >>>

His cine-camera he would lend to me.
In my imagination I would be
A great director filming epics grand.
With cardboard megaphone I'd stand
And call directions to a cast of Scouts
And Reddy Dog, who'd quite ignore my shouts.
Bribing with titbits was the only way
To get co-operation in our play.
In those days colour film was rare
So we used black and white. Our Premiere
Had plink-plonk music from a tape machine,
Invited guests to see us on the screen.
So amateur, no Oscars would be won
But making it we had a lot of fun!

Boats and the sea, hills and the farm, being a Scout
Bookbinding, courting, making films - without
Much in the way of future plans - a jolly game...

My boyhood ended when my Call-up Papers came.

GLORIA

Gloria's Transit van was her pride and joy,
  When she set off for France on Sunday
But the following morn when the Ferry docked,
  SIC TRANSIT GLORIA MUNDI. *

* (And so passes the transient glory of this world)

-----<>-----

HAREBELLS

In chapel as a child
I found a harebell, heavenly blue,
Pressed in my hymn book.
How long it had been there
I didn't know. The flower
Was thinner than the pages
Which had crushed it flat.
It was still bright
And smelt of mountains.

Towering above me,
Stern, unsmiling faces,
Dark serge suits,
Another sombre Sunday.

Dust drifted golden in the sunbeams.
Moses' rod and water gushing in the wilderness
Suddenly seemed a minor miracle
To what I knew was happening -
Outside.

Slipping unnoticed
Past the giant trousered legs,
I left.

"I like the atmosphere," I said,
"Excitement, bustle, city life, pub chatter.
London has everything!
Theatres, galleries,
Writers and artists,
History and pageantry."
What more could I desire?

Yet in my bed-sit
I could not recall a show I'd seen,
Meeting a *real* writer,
Seeing a picture that I could compare
With Mynydd Pen-y-Fal from Skirrid Fawr,
Harebells around my feet.

Slipping unnoticed
Past the giant tower blocks
I left.

-----<>-----

LARKS AND OWLS

Some men and women (of which I am one),
Rise early and are instantly awake
But energy sinks with the setting sun.
We 'larks' quite quickly to our beds then take.

But other people, rising later on,
Are bright and active far into the night.
They only tire with the darkness gone,
The pseudonym of 'owls' would seem just right.

How odd that 'larks' to 'owls' are always wed,
I've often pondered on this strange affair.
They quarrel when the other stays in bed,
Of Nature's purpose they are unaware.

Nature evolved this process of selection
So 'man cubs', in the cave, had most protection.

-----<>-----

ONE GOOD CHURN

Two frogs fell in a bowl of cream
And started swimming round and round.
"There's no way out," the weak one said,
Gave up and sank and drowned.

The other frog, of sterner stuff,
"I won't give up," was heard to utter
And went on swimming round and round,
Then hopped out from the butter.

-----<>-----

The thoughts of some are sparkling mountain streams
Reflecting sunshine, shallow, bright and clear.
No need to search for depth, just passing dreams,
Popular cliches splash and tinkle here.

The thoughts of some are merely winterbournes
In 'summer good times' empty, dried-up bores,
Each sudden storm a raging flood then spawns
And, passing, leaves just flattened grass and straws.

The thoughts of some rush through a steep ravine,
Pitted with polished holes where stones go round,
Grinding great hollows where their souls have been.
Deep in dark pools, rare gemstones may be found.

Such precious jewels should be keenly sought,
These adamantine relics of some poet's thought.

*

(Winterbourne - a stream-bed empty in summer, becoming a river in Winter, or during a storm)

KISSING HANDS

Helen
When first I saw
Your baby hand, born fingerless,
I cried and put it to my lips
A vain attempt to 'kiss it better'.

Later I learned to kiss each hand
To show I didn't mind
And let you know that every part
Was just as precious as the rest.

Now, when I watch you play
Handling each problem with such joy and zest
I kiss your hand
From sheer respect

I never notice which.

-----<>-----

MY HILL

They're going to build a wind-farm on my hill,
That hill I see across the valley now.
My hill.

They say I do not own my hill.
I have no title deeds, no legal right,
No valid interest in what they're going to do.

It's not enough to say I love that hill,
Have seen it in a thousand different moods,
Enjoyed for many years its peace, its calmness,
Its stability.

It's not enought to say I love to stand
And watch cloud shadows slide across its face
To say how I enjoy its dignity and majesty.

I will admit to being green,
Fearing Chernobyl in this pleasant land
And I was one who thought the answer must
Be blowing in the wind.

But I have seen, since then, on other people's hills,
The lines of urgent, waving, drowning arms
That crowd their distant skies.

No more will 'jocund day
Stand tiptoe on my misty mountain top'.
Instead I'll see the flailing three-armed cross
On which my peace of mind is being crucified -
And cry.

-----<>-----

HOBSON'S BUTTERFLY

Two caterpillars chomped along a leaf,
One hairy brown, one luminescent green.
Their life was one big munch - no grief
Disturbed this meal - their futures quite unseen.

A butterfly, tan, orange, red and black
Flew over, floating, tumbling in the breeze
Thrown upwards, downwards, sideways, forward, back,
Twisting and turning through the sunlit trees.

Said Luminescent Green to Hairy Brown,
"That creature's tossed by every wind that blows.
A faulty concept - wing design unsound -
You'd never get *me* up in one of those!"

-----<>-----

A DROP OF DOGGEREL

I interviewed a man last night
Who'd just come up from Tooting.
Though blind from birth, his claim to fame
Was - he loved parachuting.

I asked him how he knew the time
To brace himself for landing.
He answered with a ready smile
At my not understanding.

"It's easy, Mike," the man replied,
"I have this simple knack.
I know when I am near the ground -
My guide-dog's lead goes slack."

-----<>-----

Do you remember Uncle Taffy?
When War broke out he joined the NAAFI.
That way he'd have a cushy time.
But, drunk one night, he thought he'd climb
Aboard a bomber in a hangar
To sleep it off. Boy, what a clanger!

When he awoke from dreams so sweet,
He was at twenty thousand feet,
And on his way to bomb Berlin.
"Good God," said Taffy, "What's that din?"
The flak was bursting all about
And Taffy said, "I'm getting out."

He grabbed a 'chute, made for the door
And opened it and then, before
He realised just where he was,
He was sucked out of there, because
The slipstream caught his parachute.
His consternation was acute -
But Taffy held on tight till he
Landed, to his dismay, in Stalag Three.

Most men would say, "What rotten luck,"
But Taffy didn't give a - damn,
Just got to work upon a plan.

First to the barber - head to shave,
Donated blood - three pints Taff gave.
The dentist - all his teeth pulled out,
His nails clipped - flushed down the spout.
Stripped to the waist out in the sun
Skin peeling off when Taff was done.

A gut pain next - doctor to fix
The way, remove Taff's ap-pen-dix.
He then applied to be a Jew - don't scoff -
Though what he wanted done was, "A bit off."

Our Taff was brought before Herr Kapitan
Who said, "Vee know your little plan.
Vee've worked it out, and zis must cease.
You are escaping from here - piece by piece!"

-----<>-----

"They have no culture, they are savages."
Therefore we were quite free
To kill the men and use their women,
Corrupt their children,
Force them to fear our loving God
And make them work the 'empty' lands for us.
Firearms imposed our will.

"They have no culture, they are only whales."
Therefore we are quite free
To hunt and kill, for oil and flesh
To feed our pets and gourmet Japanese.
Call it 'Research for Science',
Pretend it's for the good of Whales.
Harpoons impose our will.

Yet now we know the 'savages'
Did have a culture, different from ours,
In tune with Nature
And the places where they lived.
But it's too late - the last sad remnants fade,
Old men and women pass away to Dreamland,
Only rock paintings and their artifacts remain.

A thousand years from now, if men exist,
Will they remember then
The gentle singing giants of the deep,
Whose culture we have failed to comprehend?
Our human brains inadequate,
Our intellects earthbound.

Instead we reach for Space.
It's there we hope to find Intelligence
As great as ours.

-----<>-----

FROM WHENCE COMETH

I need the sight of hills

They do not have to be the Himalayan 'Far Pavilions',
Though I would dearly love to stand
On rhododendron-shaded trails and see
Those mighty mountains crowd the sky.

In Africa I saw Mount Kenya shyly flash
A glimpse of equatorial snows
At dawn and dusk,
And watched the rising sun glow pink on crater rims
At nineteen thousand feet.

I've photographed the peaks and glaciers
On Alps too perfect to be real
And learned it is not size that counts
For almost any modest hill will do.

How I survived two years at Ely
In the level fens, I do not know.
My eyes would scan the distant view,
Making from clouds a fantasy
Of jumbled peaks and vaporous valleys,
Imagined mountains for an aching soul.

Now when I turn mine eyes
Unto the hills
I see the Blorenge, Pen-y-Fal and Skirrid Fawr.
No giants these,
Yet help comes forth.

Familiar outlines fill a vacant space
A pattern is complete within my mind.
I turn away and face the World
My inner strength restored.

I need the sight of hills.

-----<>-----

One summer we had hornets at the farm,
Yellow and brown, three times the size of wasps.
That know-all, Alan Pritchard, said,
"Their sting will kill a carthorse."
Scared as I was, I vowed I would locate their nest,
And burn them out.

I saw myself a saviour - to my boyish mind
I'd be Saint George, slaying a fearsome foe.
Each evening I would try and trace the route
These dreaded creatures took,
But as they flew so fast I always failed.

My brother Gareth found the answer. With a tube
Of Balsawood Cement,
We glued a feather to a hornet's back
And followed it, unwitting Judas, to the nest.

Across the dingle, into Evan's Wood,
The feather led us, to a hollow oak
Where, as we watched, its bearer entered,
Followed by others, unadorned.

We trembled where we stood,
Thinking of all the cart-horse killers in the tree.

That night we came again
With tins of petrol and a light
And, greatly daring, poured it in the hole
Then struck a match and threw that in as well.

Standing well back, we heard the sullen roar
Of fire within the trunk consume the nest
And in the glow, watched late returning workers
Flying in, get scorched and die.

We were the heroes of the hour.
I could not stay away,
Returning often in the following days
To watch the wisps of smoke
From smouldering punkwood rise,
Mixed with the ashes of a thousand virgin queens.

>>>

Forty years on, I thought I saw a hornet in my wood.
I could be wrong, it might have been a wasp
Though late, in June, to see a queen.

I hope it was a hornet,
I would hate to know I was the human
Who had put the torch
To that last remnant of an ancient race
Whose right to life was just as great as mine.

-----<>-----

MY HEDGE

My garden had a Russian privet hedge.
The leaves were yellow, not the usual green.
It was admired by my neighbours then,
So uniform, so bright and, seemingly,
So easily maintained.

But as a gardener, I found
Green, healthy shoots would sprout
Deep in the hedge. And,
Which at the time, seemed very strange to me,
The green would taint the yellow leaves nearby.

To keep the hedge the way it had been planned
I had to take my secateurs
And ruthlessly prune out these errant shoots.

One day, when doing this, I saw the maker's sign,
Engraved upon the handle of the tool -
Entwined initials, reading 'KGB'.

My garden has a Russian privet hedge.
Now it is mostly green and grows like mad,
Sprouting in all directions, making extra work.
But birds nest in it now
And hedgehogs forage round the roots.
This is the way I want my hedge to be.

-----<>-----

ARMISTICE PARADE AT ELY CATHEDRAL 1957

We stood
A hundred servicemen and girls
In uniforms of khaki and of Air Force Blue
And in our midst a single sailor, home on leave -
One volunteer, at least.

In that huge, medieval nave
We sang 'O Valiant Hearts'
And heard the Padre tell
Of 'Pastures Green' and 'Death's Dark Vale',
To honour those who fell,
In war, when we were children,
And in that other dreadful war
They called the 'Great'
Some thirty years before.

A bugle
Sounded
From the gloom
Down by the Western Door
'The Last Post' - sombre, slow and sad
Echoing
Each heavy note,
Drifting among the pillars and the tombs
To fade away and die
In corners dark.

We heard the words,
Familiar to us all,
'Age shall not weary them,
Nor years condemn'.

Then - from that same simple instrument
Sprang forth 'Reveille'.
Notes of purest gold - lighting the gloom
Darted above our heads,
Soared up
Into the massive vault of Ely's Lantern Tower
To flutter there like doves
Drawing our souls up Heavenwards. >>>

No death had been in vain!

There in my youthful innocence
I thought, 'If I should die
In some strange land,
I would not mind
If I could know
I would be thus remembered,
Every year
By bugle calls at 'Ely in the Fens'.

And then we marched back
Through the driving rain to Camp.

-----<>-----

MY DAFFODIL

One long past Spring I walked alone
    Through gloomy woods along the riverside,
And there to my surprise and joy,
    A single golden daffodil I spied.

Torn from its bed by Winter's storms
    And tossed upon the raging flood,
Its bulb then cast upon the bank
    To rot amongst the stones and mud.

The life inside would not be stilled
    Though bruised and battered by the world,
But in that cold and hostile place
    Its golden petals had unfurled.

Now daffodils may dance in hosts
    And so delight the poet's eye,
But my brave, lonely daffodil
    Will flower within me till I die.

-----<>-----

Five, four, three, two, one.
Not 'Blast off', just a gentle lift
From prototype Atomic Fusion Motors.
Swiftly we climb, Professor Melanie and I
Into Earth orbit.

When we look down,
The Earth, a globe of green and blue,
Moves past our window -
So beautiful when seen from Space.

We circle once, look down on Cape Canaveral,
It's gone!
A pool of magma, boiling rock,
Spreads outwards.

Someone has blundered -
A calculation not complete?
Computer error? Hell!
We stare aghast
And orbit on,
Remote spectators.

We circle twice.
Florida is boiling coast to coast,
The sea is steaming round a spreading ring.

Once more around.
The Southern States and Mexico
Have gone.

Each orbit more destruction.

>>>

At seventeen,
The icecaps melt
And we alone are living,
So far above what was the Earth -
Just Melanie and me.

How soon before the land can be repopulated,
Five, ten, twenty million years?
We haven't got that time,
Professor Melanie and me.

-----<>-----

PONDERING THE INFINITE

"Time always was and Time will always be,
And Space goes on forever" I am told.
My mind can't grasp these concepts,
  they are far too big for me,
I try and form a picture, but the images won't hold.

I can visualise a Decade and a Century as well
A Millennium is almost in my reach
But the idea of 'Eternity' just makes my mind rebel
And the thought breaks up and scatters
  like a shipwreck on a beach.

Primeval Man's evolving brain just didn't need to
  know
Of 'Time' beyond his threescore years and ten
And 'Distance' was a three day hunt,
  as far as he could go,
And then carry back his quarry to the den.

"Infinity - think on it," my puny brain I ask,
But the tool just isn't equal to the task.

-----<>-----

BLESS THIS HOUSE

Dusk in mid-afternoon
I raced the storm down from the sombre hills,
Hail rattling on my anorak.
Numb fingers fumbled with the mountain gate
Into a nettled yard.
Beyond it stood the house, stone roofed,
Unlived in now, but offering
Promise of shelter.

Blue painted door,
Tied with a bow of rotting binder-twine
To keep out sheep,
No barrier to me.

I stepped into the cobwebbed gloom
Of stone-flagged kitchen where,
Shivering,
I looked around.

A candle in a bottle,
Knobby with waxen drips,
Stood on a deal table.

Lighting the wick,
I saw the unswept hearth,
A rug of knotted rags,
Thick with black dog hairs, dusty.
No sign of recent life.

Hung on a nail, a calendar
Gave me my clue.
Five years had gone
Since last a sheet had been torn off,
To show 'December 1965'.

Above the fireplace
A text, in darkwood frame,
Proclaimed that 'God is Love'.
Tucked in behind the frame,
A sprig of shrivelled holly leaves,
Berries black wrinkled currants now.

A model of an eager dog,
A minor trophy,
Tarnished, with peeling silver plate,
Was on the mantelshelf.

>>>

I took it in my hand and saw
A hillside in the sun,
Low whistle heard,
Intent black dog moves forward at the crouch,
A stick extends an outstretched arm.
Sheep penned, gate closed,
Grudging applause.
I gently put it back upon the shelf.

I knew behind the corner door
I'd find a spiral stair
Within the thickness of the wall.

In flickering candlelight
I tiptoed up the worn stone steps.
A brass-knobbed bed half-filled a tiny room.
I was relieved to find no occupant,
Though on the end a pair of trousers hung,
And mildewed boots stood, waiting, on the floor.

Above the bed another text said
'Bless This House'.

Going downstairs, I sensed the grief
Of dying alone at Christmas.
No woman there to tidy up,
No family to take the farm in hand.

How long before the dog, unwittingly,
Had told a neighbour of his master's death
By scavenging in hunger
At their door?

A shaft of amber sunlight lit the room.
I stepped out, into clean-washed air,
Putting to flight a magpie from the yard,
And left the unblessed house.

I hope God loved the shepherd.
I had seen no sign that others did -
Except,
Perhaps,
The dog.

-----<>-----

Adapted from a story by Laurens Van der Post

A night in Africa.
Above - the stars hang bright.
Not far away, a lion coughs and grunts.
A fire burns, lighting a ring of faces round about,
Making the velvet blackness darker still.

I was a guest.
My hosts a bushman family.
This desert was their home
And had been for a million years.
I sat amongst them and I heard this tale:

Once, long ago,
A hunter, drinking at a dawn-bright pool,
Saw the reflection of a great, white bird,
But, when he raised his head,
The bird was gone.

He drank again, then rising
Followed to the north,
Leaving behind his home, his family,
His hunting ground, the lands he knew so well,
All that was dear to him.

For years he searched in vain,
Then, old and weak,
He reached a cliff impossible to climb
But he was told that, at the top,
Was this bird's nest.

As he looked up,
A single feather, white,
Came floating down
And landed in his hand. >>>

He died there, on that rock,
Content.

And here the story ended.
A woman threw a log upon the fire,
Sparks flying up, twisted towards the stars.
I turned, a question on my lips:
"This bird," I asked, "What was it called?"

The wizened bushman who had told the tale, said,
"In our legends it has many names.
In all my dreams
It is the Bird of Truth."

-----<>-----

A poet looks for -

Not just the bare facts but the

Underlying Truth

-----<>-----

Poets just express

What other people feel - but

Can't articulate.

Poets must express

What other people feel - but

Can't articulate.

-----<>-----

HANDS UP FOR A THIRD MILLENNIUM

Only the whales and dolphins have evolved
A bigger brain than ours
But we have hands -
Hands for manipulating tools
For holding pens or brushes,
Instruments for saving life
Or guns for taking it.

Forests of air-renewing trees
Scream with the bite of power saws.
We see on every hand
Quarries and roads erode
Thyme-scented hills.

Oceans, at one time vibrant with the songs
Of many whales
Are handy sumps
To catch the effluents of affluence.

We cannot hand ten million beavers back
Their stolen skins
Retusk dead elephants
Rehorn a rotting rhino's skull.....

Recall how
In the First Millennium
People around the world took
Only what they needed then
To live from hand to mouth.

In the next
We let our arrogance and greed
Skin, scalp, eviscerate and poison this
So handsome planet - Earth.

And now, hands reaching out
We race into a new Millennium.

Slap, slap these grasping, errant hands of ours
And make us worthy of a Third.

A FLY IN AMBER

Ten million years ago a fly
Mistakenly
Landed on resin weeping from a wounded tree,
Was trapped and,
As the tree wept on,
Encapsulated,
Perfectly preserved.

Was this an ordinary fly
The same as others of its time?
We have no way to judge
For just this one
Was fossilised.
I hold it here,
In amber,
Perfectly preserved.

Ten million million words are uttered every day.
Which will survive the predators of time?
It may be those that have been trapped
When wounded Mankind wept.
"Father, forgive them,"
"Et tu, Brute?" "To be or not to be,"
"We'll fight them on the beaches." Words like these
Will live on,
Perfectly preserved.

But who will make the final choice?
Which word or phrase
Will be the fly that only briefly flew,
But acts as representative,
Encapsulated,
Perfectly preserved?

If I could name a single phrase or word
That might survive ten million years,
Trapped in the amber wept by Man,
It would be: "While there's Life, there's Hope"
Or simply,
"Hope."
Either would do - if
Perfectly preserved.

-----<>-----

Below the Darren, where the ravens nest,
Half hidden in a sheltered dell,
A long abandoned shepherd's cottage stood
And here we children of Cwm Cadno played at 'house'.

Although the rooms were open to the sky
We didn't care, or even notice, this
We'd light a fire in the old stone hearth
For boiling hedge-laid eggs
And baking dough.

We called the long-dead shepherd Sam,
His wife was Jane, and sometimes we were they.
At other times we called ourselves their children,
Helping with lambing, shearing, making hay
And tying bags of raddle to the tup.

Poking around amongst the stones
As children do, I found a broken plate,
Well hidden in a secret place.
China so thin and delicate that,
When I held it up against the sun,
I saw the outline of my fingers clear
Though on the other side.

Porcelain patterned with flowers, red and blue,
Around the edge a ring of gleaming gold.
I held the pieces in my hand,
Enchanted.

I was alone that day and,
Seated on a stone, holding the shards
I saw a scene so real
It must have been.

A child had taken down the plate
From off the dresser where it stood,
Jane's pride and joy, a wedding gift from Gran.
On climbing down, had slipped
And dropped the purloined treasure
To the floor. >>>

The child and Jane were crying, Sam came in,
Tired and hungry from the hill.
He roughly took the pieces from Jane's hands
And threw them in the midden,
"Useless now."

The picture darkened. I saw Jane,
Holding a lantern, find the broken bits
And hide them in the place I'd found,
Out of Sam's sight.

I took the pieces home to show to Mam.
Megan, who knew about these things,
Or thought she did, said it was very old,
And rare, and had it been complete
Would have been worth
"A bob or two."

I kept them for a week,
Whilst I enjoyed the colour and the silky feel
Of antique porcelain, then took them back.
They still belonged to Jane.

Last year, I poked about, as adults do,
In Portobello Road
And found a plate, identical to Jane's.
But perfect, not a chip nor crack.
I bought it, though it cost
More than "A bob or two"
And took it home,
Safe in a padded box.

Only the ravens know where it is now.

Today, when Mary asked
"Where is that plate you bought?"
I said, "It must be in the attic.
Look! There's a polly wagtail on the lawn.
Look - over there."

-----<>-----

THE PAPER BOY

Pity the Paper Boy in Winter
Trudging the streets in pre-dawn darkness,
Sludge splashed by passing cars,
Glimpses of families at breakfast,
Remote in cosy kitchens.
Headlines all gloom and doom.
Pity the Paper Boy in Winter,
Driven by greed, or need.

Envy the paper Boy in Summer,
When sun lights up the quiet streets.
Cycling illicitly on pavements,
Watching the early birds,
Greeting the joggers.
How trivial the headlines now.
Envy the Paper Boy in Summer.
All this - and pocket-money, too.

-----<>-----

A PARADOX

From Lulworth Cove to Kimmeridge the Army owns the land,
And it's here that soldiers practice killing men.
For years they wired off the range, and you and I were banned
For only guns and tanks had access then.

From Kimmeridge to Lulworth Cove the Army was 'the boss'
And the only things to plough the ground were tanks.
The houses and the gardens were submerged in weeds and moss
And bracken, ferns and brambles hid the banks.

From Lulworth Cove to Kimmeridge the Army's dropped its guard,
And, just sometimes, they will let the public through.
Here we marvel at the wildlife that abounds in every yard
Where no pesticides have poisoned with their soil-polluting brew.

In the battle for survival, should you be a caterpillar,
It's the Army who protects you, it's the farmer who's the killer.

-----<>-----

They call us '**black**'. Perhaps we seem that way,
When from a distance viewed, across the Wye,
But those who know our moods from day to day
Will say a name like that is just a lie.

In Spring and Summer we are many shades of green,
In Autumn, yellow, russet brown and gold,
In Winter, often white with snow we're seen,
But '**black**' - well, sometimes - if the truth be told.

-----<>-----

THE HUMAN CANNON-BALL

When Granville's Splendid Circus came to town,
It came with horses, elephants, a clown,
And acts to hold the audience in thrall.
The best of these: 'The Human Cannon-ball'.

A little man was Jim, and round -
Trusty, reliable and sound.
He'd been with Old Man Granville many years.
To lose him was the least of Granville's fears.

Each night the drum would roll as Jim would climb
Into the cannon's mouth and in a second's time,
A bang, a cloud of smoke and Jim would jet
Across the ring, land safely in the net.

His fame was legion, people came
From far and near, Jim's other name -
'The Human Cannon-ball', brought special glory
To Granville's Circus - hence this little story.

A rival Circus Master - call him Ben -
Persuaded Jim to join him in the end
By offering a wage so sumptuous
That even loyal Jim could not refuse.

When Jim told Granville he was going soon
Granvile said, "Pack up this afternoon,
I'm sorry you are leaving us behind,
Men of your calibre are hard to find."

-----<>-----

The Mount of Olives
Night, woodsmoke on the warm breeze,
A peaceful place this.

"Watch and pray with me,"
Jesus asks of them. In vain -
For, tired out, they sleep.

Jesus, restless, prays,
His back against a tree-trunk,
Hands in his lap now.

Lanterns prick darkness,
Muffled voices, clash of swords,
Soldiers are coming.

To betray Jesus,
False Judas chooses a kiss
The symbl of Love.

Swords strike, an ear bleeds.
"Who lives by the sword," Christ says,
"Shall die by the sword."

Fear overcomes love.
Disciples scatter, run off,
Hide in the darkness.

From Gethsemene,
Mark, deserting his Master,
Fleeing, runs naked.

"I'll not deny you,"
Peter swears, meaning every word.
Then the dawn cock crows.

-----<>-----

THE ABACUS OF GOD

I stood upon the mighty Chesil Bank,
For mile on mile the sea-churned pebbles ground.
Each stone a boulder was before it sank
But waves and time have made them pebbles round.

Each man is born a sharp and jagged stone,
Life knocks the corners off us all, until
Into our own appointed place we're thrown
With others, yet an individual.

Perhaps it is a cosmic counting frame,
A pebble scores the life of one good man.
The Tally Roll of Heaven ~ in God's game,
A marker for each one who kept to plan.

It wasn't just a shingle beach I trod.
I stood upon the Abacus of God.

-----<>-----

THE CHURCH BY THE LAKE

The wind of Spring was singing in the churchyard pines,
Wavelets were sparkling, dancing in the sun.
The heavy door swung open to my push.
Inside was silence.

In this House of God,
I prowled about,
Reading the tablets on the wall,
The Roll of Honour, names
Of men who left their lakeside homes
To die.
The flowers from Sunday last
Fading and drooping here, today. >>>

Near to the door, a book invited me:
PLEASE PRAY FOR THESE...
'A mother, very ill.'
'A child dying of leukaemia.'
'People of Bosnia,
Sudan, Somalia.'
A catalogue of human grief.
Not praying, I read on,
My vision blurred,
'A son on drugs.'
'A missing daughter, gone from home
To God knows where.'

I closed the book
And turned to look along the quiet nave
To where a cross gleamed gold.

The heavy door swung open to my pull.

The wind of Spring was singing in the churchyard pines,
Wavelets were sparkling, dancing in the sun.
A mallard flew a cross across the sky,
Marsh marigolds heaped mounds of treasure round my feet.
A pair of swallows, following blind instinct all the way
From Africa, swooped past.
A buzzard mocked me, mewing overhead.
Then, on the wind of Spring,
I heard God crying in a curlew's call.

-----<>-----

You will be much loved,
No matter what else you lack,
If you are just kind.

If you are just kind,
No matter what else you lack,
You will be much loved.

-----<>-----

FEELING WELSH

I was just ten years old
When first I came to Wales.
English by birth and parentage,
Of Scottish ancestry,
And even now I am betrayed by accent -
Vowels broad. 'Apples' and 'castle' are two words
Which label me a Dorset man. Yet I feel now
More Welsh than English.

The men of science tell
That water makes the greater part of us,
Ninety per cent or so.
If this is true my body must be largely Welsh
From water drunk or bathed in.
Wales absorbed in liquid form.
But no, it isn't this
Or all the Brummies would feel Welsh as well.

Or is it the language then?
It can't be that.
I only have a smattering, enough
To translate names of places on a map.

Knowledge of history and legend?
No, the Mabinogion I cannot follow through.
Llewellyn and Glyndwr are little more than names
And 'Modern Culture Wales'
Seems full of English-haters,
Poets filled with maudlin thoughts
Of mining dereliction and
'The rape of Wales',
Or obscene ranters.

Can it be The Song?
I love to hear 'Myfanwy' but I cannot sing,
Have never heard a male voice choir in the flesh,
Though once I passed a well-known Rugby ground
And heard ten thousand singing Sospan Fach'.

If there is something that has made me feel Welsh,
It must be hiding in the Hills.
An emanation from the ground absorbed when walking?

>>>

Something implanted in the ear
By skylarks, curlews, ravens, doves?
Patterns of skylines viewed, imprinted
On the brain? Or scents -
Crushed bracken, soil steaming in the sun
Or woodsmoke drifting on the evening breeze?
Tasted, perhaps, in blackberries or mountain whins
Or water sipped at moss-draped springs
High up where sheep and rugged ponies graze?
The Hills of Wales have subtly drugged and captured me,
An Englishman,
Who feels Welsh.

-----<>-----

BASHER B

We were a rotten class.
We felt it was our task
To bait new Masters,
Testing their resolve.

Then came a bearded man
With sandalled feet - oh, joy,
A lamb to sacrifice.
What sport - what fun we'd have.

He played us as a weasel plays a bird
Letting us gambol round behind his back
Pretending not to see our clumsy mimicry -
And then he pounced.

A clear transgressor
Seen, identified, called out
To stand before the class,
Dumb, insolent.

The Master reached
Deep in a pocket, found a knife
And gave it to the boy.

>>>

"Go to that privet bush outside," he said,
"And cut a stick.
A thick one, or a thin -
That is your only choice."

Now this was something new!
We waited breathless in that quiet room.
Dust drifted slow
All sounds were muted, muffled, still.

The boy returned,
Shamefaced and apprehensive.
Swish - swish - swish -
Game, set and match.

We sat in silence, listening as
'Basher' read from Wordsworth -
Michael's tale,
About a half-built sheepfold
High on Greenhead Ghyll.
I smelt the sheep's wool
And the bracken in the sun,
Felt lichen-crumbs on stones
And heard a skylark singing in that dusty room
That was no longer there.

I would not, could not, dare not,
Wanted not
To idle in this class.
Here was a Master
And a Man.

Some forty years of growth
Have passed since then.
The seeds he sowed,
Close to that cane,
Are coming to fruition -
Thanks to Basher B.

That Nom de Guerre
Is now a Chant d'amour.

---<>---

The Song of ELEGANCE OF ROCKALL -

from 'Dolphinsong'

When I was born the sun-lit, sparkling Sea
Patterned the seabed, light delighting me.
Sun, Sea, companionship and joy were mine
Grace, beauty, love and peace would intertwine
As kelp-weed in a swirling current's flow.
Now - what is the life I know?

All I possess is here within my brain
I have no hands to grasp and hold and claim.
But human hands once cast a subtle net
Unseen, unheard, unechoing, and yet
Strong to ensnare, to capture and enslave
This spirit born for Sea-life, wind and wave.

For I was taught that Dolphins love all Men
And Men love us, but now I wonder when
Their arrogance and greed this concept killed -
Still whales and dolphins die. My soul is filled
With alien emotions. Fear and hate
Pollute my mind - a toxic stream in spate.

I am a symbol of all whales' plight
Captured or killed, not knowing how to fight.
Trapped here, I swim in circles and a hatred grows.
I yearn for freedom where the sea-wind blows.
Don't let a hate for Mankind poison me.
~Yegods~ and little fishes - set me free.

-----<>-----

The Song of GRACE OF FAIR ISLE 39

from 'Dolphinsong'

I, Fair Isle, call to Thinking Men -
See us for what we are.

Not competition for your fish
Not fools to entertain your young
Not handy hulks of oil and flesh
But creatures of intelligence
A Nation of our own,
Deserving something better from
Our one-time friends
Who occupy dry portions of this planet
You call Earth
But which is mostly Sea.

We know that you have eyes to see
And ears to hear.
We know that you have brains to think.
We know imagination flourishes in men.
We hope that you have souls
To feel compassion, too.

Please use your hands to signal
STOP
And let us live.

See us for what we are:
A peaceful, gentle Nation of the Sea.

-----<>-----

MY BROTHER TIM

My brother Tim makes poetry
But as machines.
Where I use words and rhymes,
Tim uses nuts and bolts,
Milled plastic blocks,
Electric motors,
Tiny gears and cogs
And PCB's, in combinations
Mystical to me,
A minor wordsmith.

I know I must refine my thoughts,
Condense, compress,
Make every word a working part
That makes a contribution to the whole.
If any poem I create
Is rough or clumsy, then
It just won't do for me.

Tim is the same:
Unspoiled by education,
With a mind original in thought,
Bold in conception,
Delicate in detail,
He creates machines
To change our money,
Handle coins or notes,
Do anything you ask.

If you've a need:
Mechanical, electrical
Or electronic - Tim
Can soon design and build
Some thing to do the job.

But not just anything
To do it crudely.
What he will make will be
Compact and fuctional,
Contained within a stylish case,
The minimum of moving parts.

>>>

Quite probably a unique way
To use some Rule of Physics
In a way not done by anyone before.

The pride with which he shows it off
Is just as great as mine
When you allow me time
To read to you a poem I've composed.
I'd like to think we both create
Devices -
Each to fill a need
With Elegance.

-----<>-----

CASTELL CADNO

Ten years ago, deep in the hills,
I found a castle, time-decayed,
Hidden amongst the birches and the pines,
So far from any human track,
It was forgotten and, praise be,
Unknown to Cadw and the National Trust.

The walls were crumbling,
Stones were loose and dangerous,
Adventure lurked up every spiral stair.
No concrete capping, handrails, hidden lights,
Only sad ghosts and Romance lingered there.

A gang of jackdaws quarrelled in the long-cold stacks
And ring-doves coo'd from ivy-hidden nests,
Ferns filled the dungeons,
In the gloom, I heard the groans of English knights,
Glendower's unwilling guests.

>>>

Where dark-eyed Morfydd once had barred her door
To thwart a prince's lust, I stood

And through her empty window
Watched a tired sun
Slide down behind Bryn Cadno. In the dusk

A fieldmouse sat and preened its whiskers
Unafraid of me, a human form
More solid than the shapes it mostly saw
Walking those rooms at nightfall.

A breeze through mullioned windows blew
Chill, swirling dead leaves
Around the stone-flagged floor.
A silent owl wafted across the yard,
A stone fell from the tower wall.

My arms were nettles to my fingertips
My hair was bristles on a brush.
Not looking back, I left.

Beyond, a pair of pipistrelle
Weaving cats-cradles in between the trees
Ignored me, hurrying below.

Climbing the ridge, I slowed my pace
Then, looking back,
Sought out the tower above the trees.
The gleam of light I thought I saw
Could only be a chance reflection from the sky,
The scream, a vixen's call.

Until this day, I never told a soul
About my castle.

THE SECRET OF THE UNIVERSE

A song lyric

A Bushman stood on the gleaming sand
On the shore of Walvis Bay
And he called to the whales that had swum past there
For a million years and a day
And he called to the whales that had swum past there
For a million years and a day.

For he was the last of the Bushman Race,
And little and old was he
But his people had failed in their mission
To pass on the Word from the Sea.

For the Whales had worked out the Hidden Theme
That had always eluded Man
And they wanted to share with the dominant race
The Universal Plan.

They had learned to speak to the Bushman there
In whistles and grunts and clicks
A language common to Whales and Men -
Those little brown men with their sticks.

The Bushmen had tried to pass it on -
The World just would not hear
For what could a primitive savage know
That Science had not made clear?

On the twenty-first day a whale came
And swam in alone from the sea.
"You called me, my friend?" she said to the man.
The Last of the Whales was she.
"You called me, my friend?" she said to the man.
The Last of the Whales was she.

"That wonderful secret you told to us
Is now only here, in my head,
For the very last one of the Bushmen am I,
The rest of my kind are dead."

>>>

"And I am the last of the Whale kind,
We **must** find a way to pass on
The Secret known only to you and to me
Before you and I are gone."

"We have tried our best. I can do no more
For the World is deaf with conceit.
I'm weary now and I'm coughing blood.
Farewell, my Friend of the Sea."

The Last of the Whales then turned away
To swim to the ocean vast
At the mouth of the bay - a Whaling Ship,
A red-sun flag at its mast.

The vultures pecked out the Bushman's eyes
Hyenas gnawed at his feet
And in Tokyo the gourmets dined
On the Last of the Whale's meat.

The President strolled on the White House lawn
In a far off, mighty land
And talked with the head of NASA there
And learned of the space-flights planned.

"One day we'll fly off to worlds unknown
In that great expanse called 'Space'
And we'll look for intelligent beings there
And we'll build us a study base."

"We'd have to work their language out
And find some way to converse."
"Who knows," he quipped, "They might have found
The Secret of the Universe."
"Who knows," he quipped, "They might have found
The Secret of the Universe."

-----<>-----

Chesil Beach

Today there is no wind.
The sea breathes deep and slow
Wet pebbles nudge each other, steal a kiss
And chuckle at their daring.
Portland lies, a lazy dog, facing the land,
Its nose between its paws.
The gulls, disconsolate
Sit bored along the ridge,
Peck at their toes.
Today there is no wind.

Today the wind is in the East.
Waves quarrel, run ashore, then
Change their minds, draw back.
The pebbles groan,
Clatter and tinkle,
Knock their neighbours, try to get away
Give up, surrender, nestle down.
Bright Portland sniffs the air, alert.
Gulls ride the waves off-shore and wait,
This won't last long.
Today the wind is in the East.

Today the wind is in the West.
Green breakers tower, check,
Hold their breath, crash down - to be devoured
By those that roar and chase behind.
Bruised pebbles scream and churn
Grinding their neighbours and themselves.
No pause - see, here's a plank - toss it ashore -
This stone is bigger - pass it on. Now -
Pass it on along
Towards where wind-whipped Portland cowers,
Half-hidden by smoking spray.
Above, the gulls float joyously
White wings outstretched,
Tracing the contours of the living beach.
Alive, alive. Alive today.

Today the wind is in the West
And I am here, sea-salt upon my lips,
Alive.

I'm Joseph - just a carpenter,
Come up to Bethlehem to pay my tax.
Last night my wife gave birth.
I should be glad but no -
That baby lying over there,
He isn't mine.

I thought I heard a singing in the hills
An angel choir? It must have been a dream!
I was so tired from travelling and helping Mary through.
I should be glad - but no
That baby lying over there,
He isn't mine.

The straw on which he lies is clean and sweet
Sweet as the oxen's breath that warms this cave
Better than at the over-crowded inn.
I should be glad - but no
That baby lying over there,
He isn't mine.

The shepherds came with lambs. How did they know?
Is nothing private in these little towns?
Good fellows - honest working men like me.
I should be glad - but no
That baby lying over there,
He isn't mine.

Three rich men came and left him presents -
Gold and frankincense and myrrh
As if he were a prince. This puzzles me.
I should be glad - but no
That baby lying over there,
He isn't mine.

While Mary slept I went and looked into the child's eyes
Eager and bright - though with a sadness too
His hand clasped round my finger - very tight
And I was glad, so glad.

This baby lying in my arms
He's mine -
And yours -
And everyone's.

NOW AND THEN

(In Memorium)

Now
When you see a squirrel on a branch
Hear pigeons coo, woodpeckers drum,
Just pause and say
"He loved all this."

Now
When you see cloud-shadows slide across a sunlit hill
Feel waves crash on a pebble beach
Look around and say
"How he loved that."

Now
When you walk beside a mountain stream
Or watch a river glide past time-smoothed stones
Toss in a twig and say
"He would swim here."

Now
When you see a reed-mace tall
Its head in sun, its roots in glorious mud
Laugh at a memory and say
"He would be that."

Then
If you should hear a lonely curlew's cry
Drift, bubbling, down the wind
Listen and say
"Does anyone remember Whatsisname?"

---<>---

Evocative sound,
Heard on sun dappled mountains,
A curlew calling.

---<>---

Michael Tod
January, 1997

The poem 'Joseph's Child' may be used without further reference in any appropriate way, eg. read during a church service or reproduced in a parish magazine.

It may also be used as a script for a nativity play for younger children who may act the parts whilst the poem is read by someone else.

If reprinted in a magazine, etc. a copy of the publication would be appreciated if sent to the publishers at:

Cadno Books,
PO Box 34,
Abergavenny
NP8 1YN

A BAG OF MIXED KERNELS

by

MICHAEL TOD

To write a Kernel -
Find, distil, encapsulate
A thought that moves you.

-----<>-----

A Kernel cannot
Be quoted out of context,
Each one is complete

-----<>-----

If you think you can,
Or if you think you cannot,
Either way, you're right.

-----<>-----

It is a pity
That Noah could not resist
A unicorn steak.

-----<>-----

A poet's message
Should be wrapped in cellophane,
Clever wraps obscure.

-----<>-----

Beautiful rosebuds
So exquisite in themselves
Promise even more.

-----<>-----

Most satisfying -
Good done by stealth, discovered
Accidentally.

-----<>-----

The scent of woodsmoke
Caught unexpectedly, stirs
Pleasant memories.

-----<>-----

If you are lucky
And have a whole loaf, sell half
And buy a lily.

-----<>-----

Hot water bottles
Modest, unassuming things,
Comforters supreme.

-----<>-----

When work overwhelms,
A thousand things must be done -
Go climb a mountain.

-----<>-----

Fishing is enjoyed
More by anglers than by fish,
Even less by worms.

-----<>-----

The longest distance
Walked between any two points
Is called a short cut.

-----<>-----

North Cones warn of storms,
Triangular sandwiches -
Beware visitors.

-----<>-----

Love, like a good wine
Can mature as it ages -
But bottles stay firm.

-----<>-----

Successful people -
Those who get up one more time
Than they are knocked down.

-----<>-----

Going through the mill,
In some strange way, releases -
Creativity.

-----<>-----

Fear knocked at the door
Courage went to answer it
And no-one was there.

-----<>-----

Is love pure magic,
Or a genetic signal
To trigger new life?

-----<>-----

Punctuality
Goes unappreciated.
Nobody is there.

-----<>-----

Migrating sea birds
Don't fly alone. One good tern
Deserves another.

-----<>-----

There is always one
Strangely evasive teaspoon
Lurking in the sink.

-----<>-----

Inflation arrived
Using Decimal coinage
As a Trojan Horse.

-----<>-----

Rainbows, kingfishers
And happiness - don't stay long.
Each a fleeting joy.

-----<>-----

A secret pleasure
Sitting on a toilet seat
Warm from one you love.

-----<>-----

If you just knew all
Then you would understand all
Then you'd forgive all.

-----<>-----

True security
Comes from the acceptance of
Insecurity.

-----<>-----

Faroese people
Love their gentle pilot whales -
Grilled, medium rare.

-----<>-----

It is more noble
To give a book, than lend one -
The cost is the same.

-----<>-----

CWM CADNO DAYS

by

MICHAEL TOD

CWM CADNO DAYS

by

Michael Tod

Memories of childhood on a hill farm in Wales.

My family at Cwm Cadno:

'Da' Price	My father
Mam	My mother
Megan	My grown-up sister
Dai	My elder brother
Huw Price	Myself
Gareth	My younger brother

The stories: Page

A Shot in the Dark 1
Cherry Plums 2
Pigeon Pair 3
Duration Model 4
Eels 5
A Good Show 6
Fences 7
Better Than a Parrot 8
Cockles and Icecream 9
The New Way 11
Witty Bits 12
Aphrodite 13
The Vacuum 15
Mixed Posies 16
Lost Magic 17

A SHOT IN THE DARK 1

One night we stood, three boys and Da, under a starry sky, frost nipping our fingers. Megan and Mam inside, knitting by the fire.

"Bloodthirsty lot, you," Mam said, but knowing the rats must die.

Our boots rustled the leaves. We saw the hen-house, silent and dark, across the farmyard. I felt the cord, taut as a bowstring. Death at my fingertips.

That afternoon we'd driven a stake, lashed the Twelvebore and sighted, with infinite care, along the feed-trough. The cord to the trigger now vibrated to my touch. I pulled, gently. Executioner. Death by firing squad.

A blue flame stabbed at the night. A charge of Eley Number Six raking the grain thieves. The shot echoing around the silent hills.

A squeal of pain - dying. Drowned by a cacophony of clucking from hens awakened.

We ran across the yard, Da strode behind. Light on. Not one or two: six dead - our hopes exceeded.

Picking up corpses cautiously, by scaly tails, we pitched the bodies callously into the midden. The hens, unheeding, thinking it was day, pecked sleepily in the blood-spattered trough.

Petty gods, we reload. Lightning to strike twice. It seemed so easy.

"Give them an hour."

Minutes passing slowly. Clock ticking loudly. Da winds it; not even Sunday.

Once more, we rustled the leaves and pulled the cords of death. No squeals this time. Squawking and flapping wings.

"Dear God," said Da, hand on the switch. "Your Mam will kill us."

Ten hens, caught by the darkness, had roosted on the trough edge. Taking this charge. Not a single rat to justify the carnage. Downy fluff, small feathers, floated on air. We stood, four gawping fools, dreading Mam's tongue.

"To market - full of pellets? There'd be talk in Chapel. Those Price boys, shooting at chickens now."

That was ten days gone. I'd murder for a slice of pork.

Walking one evening by the river with Alan Pritchard, we were hungry. (Boys always are) Playing 'ducks and drakes' at the shallows, Alan said, "Cherry plums," and my mouth watered. Only one tree in our district, maybe the world. I've never seen others.

Morgan's Orchard - no-one about there. I climb. Alan watches.

Do you remember 'windcheaters'? Anoraks, they call them now. But these had 'lastic making a waistband and a zipper up the front. Just right for scrumping.

The fruit was ready, ripe and juicy. Zip down a bit, dozens of cherry plums filling the front. Looked like I was pregnant.

Reaching out for one last temptress, the branch breaking, me falling. Thump on the ground. Sick, dizzy, in pain, awful, something broken. I lie there, groaning.

Alan goes for Morgan. He comes running. Out of breath, Old Morgan. Helps me to stand up, arm paining something dreadful.

In Mrs Morgan's kitchen, on the settle, drinking tea, me. Hot and sweet. "For shock," says Mrs Morgan.

Old Doctor Griffiths, summoned, comes in his Wolseley, upright and black (the car, not Doctor) He is bald and stooping. Gentle, but a terror to the workshy. They say he gives out sicknotes like it hurts him.

He feels my arm. "Jacket off, I think," says Doctor, undoing my zipper.

Cherry plums! Cascading, bouncing and rolling across the floor and under the table.

Alan Pritchard blushing, colour of cherry plums. Me, ashamed, then. "Sorry," I mumble.

Mrs Morgan gets a basket.

Me to the 'Cottage', wrapped in a blanket, arm to be plastered. Mam and Da visit.

"Apologies needed," says Mam.

"Reparations," says Da. "Not money, too easy. A day muck-spreading, for Morgan. That should do it."

"When your arm's better, of course," said Mam quickly.

Mrs Morgan sent some fruit: black grapes, bananas, apples and a pear, in a chip basket. No cherry plums.

Thank you, Mrs. Morgan.

-----<>-----

PIGEON PAIR 3

My friend, Alan Pritchard, kept pigeons. 'Homers', he called them. Very special, he told me. You could take them anywhere in the world, release them and they would fly home, unerringly. Magic. I wanted one. Or two. Then they would breed and I would have more 'homers'.

Dai said I could make a fortune with just two. Selling them over and over. But I knew he was joking.

Saving my pocket money through the Winter, come Spring, Alan showed me the nest of his pigeons. Just a few twigs and two white eggs. Like chickens' only smaller and rounder. My pigeons in them.

Later, he showed me the babies, 'squabs' he called them. So ugly, covered in blood quills. Not sleek and handsome like their parents.

"They will be," Alan promised.

I named them Arno and Peggy when I bought them from Alan.

I made a cage to keep them until they knew that our farm their home was. To come back to - always.

Special food to buy, with wheat and maize in, and beans, for my pigeons.

Alan told me they must be strong for flying, over oceans and mountains. Racing to come home to Cwm Cadno.

Pretty birds now. Feathers glossy, reflecting the light in 'irridescence' as Alan called it.Their cooing - like porridge boiling.

Next came training. Each day I would take them further down the meadow before releasing. Watch them come flying back to the home I'd made them. **My** homers.

Came the Big Day for releasing my pigeons out of sight of Cwm Cadno. Me with Gareth, carrying Arno and Peggy in boxes down the valley. Dai waiting, to time them, flying home. Over two miles.

Box open, Arno and Peggy bursting into the sky. Wings clapping, climbing in circles, getting their bearings, to fly back to Cwm Cadno. Higher and higher, tiny specks now.

But, I'm sorry, I have to tell you, I never saw my 'homers', ever again.

-----<>-----

I saw an advert in a comic, for a kit for making a model aircraft. Seven shillings and twopence (including postage).

I had a postal order from Christmas, for seven and sixpence.

'Dear Sirs, Please send model kit, enclosed is postal order. Yours sincerely, Huw Price, Cwm Cadno. PS: you can keep the change.'

Dear Master Price, Your kit is enclosed herewith. Your kind offer about the fourpence we are not allowed to accept, so we are sending some extra transfers.'

Sticks of balsa, tissue paper, a propeller, wire and wheels, a tin with dope in, and a tube of balsawood cement. Also a plan, and some instructions for how to make it.

Dai helping, I build the model, smooth the propeller with sandpaper (all provided). Stick on tissue, wrinkly, disappointing. Paint the dope on, smelling of peardrops, gently.

Drying, the tissue tightens, smooth and glossy. Smashing! Now the transfers. And the 'lastic through the middle.

Winding the propeller twists the 'lastic. Let go - propeller whirling. Model, pulling forward.

Now for testing, in the garden. Get the balance exactly.

With Dai and Gareth, up the meadow to fly it. I carry the model so carefully, not to break it.

By the top hedge, winding and winding the propeller, until ready for flying.

Launch it - as instructed - into the wind. Flying lovely, in a circle, climbing.

Power finished. Plane gliding down now. Landing in the next field - with the heifers.

Silly creatures make a circle round it, sniffing and nudging.

Gareth running, chasing heifers.

In a contest - heifers' hooves versus balsawood and tissue paper, only one winner. No repairing.

I was heartbroken (for an hour). Then, up the mountain with Gareth, looking for birds' nests.

-----<>-----

One evening, early in Summer, I went to the river for swimming.

Other boys from the village were undressing in the bushes.

In the water, I could see, was something unusual, looking like a rope, twisting, just under the surface. It was elvers, thousands of elvers, wriggling and swimming up the river, in a column as thick as my arm was.

The other boys swimming just ignored them where they were splashing and shouting in the water. Me, I forgot swimming. I went walking the riverside. No break in the column, upstream or downstream. Just thousands and millions of elvers.

Where the boys were, the elvers had scattered, reforming the column further upriver.

Where had they come from? Where were they going?

All that night, I saw elvers, swimming in millions, through my dreaming.

Come morning, I go down to the river, but not an elver. Perhaps I had been......just dreaming.

At school, tell all about it to Fanny (as we called her). Really, she was Mrs Biology Jones, Teacher. Always interested in what I told her, was Fanny.

In the library was a book on fishes. I read: 'Eels breed in the ocean. In the Sargasso, under the seaweed. Millons of elvers swimming to Europe, find rivers to swim up.' Just like I saw them.

'Most get eaten by something. Just one from a million grows big, returning to the Sargasso, for mating.'

Every winter, when the floods come, the river rises, cutting corners and leaving pools there.

Trout and eels, sometimes a salmon, get trapped there. No escaping. Hiding under branches, rafts of driftwood, in tin-cans and long-drowned wellies.

Often in evenings, come the summer, I went fishing in the flood pools. (Not allowed to in the river) Taking worms from near the muckheap. Juicy, tempting, trout can't resist them, nor can eels.

Except the Monster.

>>>

A huge one in the Big Pool, must be six foot, maybe seven. Body - like a bike tyre. Eyes red, glowing, he used to watch me as I dangled fat worms, hook hidden, only inches from his snout. He just ignored them.

Tempted? He must be, but never biting.

Every evening for a fortnight, I tried for 'Monster'. Always failing to catch him.

I made a spear then - to spike him. After that I never saw him. Wise old bugger.

That one Summer, we had a cloudburst up the valley. Sudden flooding washed the pools through.

The Monster? Gone - to the Sargasso, for mating, under the seaweed.

So now there would be more elvers in the river.

A sort of circle: round and round, like, on and on, like, forever.

-----<>-----

A GOOD SHOW

From Cwm Cadno we could look down to the Showground in the valley. One day each summer a big Show was held there.

Cattle and horses, sheep and goats, dogs and rabbits competing for honours.

Mam and Megan would enter sponge-cakes and home-made jam in contests. Sometimes winning.

The marquee, with trestle tables laden with honey, gleaming in the tent-filtered sunlight, and veggies, piled in mountains, each one perfect. Apples polished, and the flowers, massed banks of colour, their scent overwhelming trapped by the hot canvas.

Mostly the sun shone on Show Day, but one year it was soaking. It rained all day, never stopping. Paths and roadways so muddy. Never seen so many umbrellas and wellies in my life as that day. Even Gentry, wading and splashing.

The farmers, flat caps and gaiters, cursing the weather, leading the cattle round the show-ring. The prize bull, massive, mean-eyed and curly-headed, slipping and sliding.

Cars sinking to their axles trying to leave the ringside.

Da told Dai to get the tractor and a tow-rope.

>>>

Our tractor was a 'Fergie', small when compared with a Fordson Major, but it could plough in places you wouldn't dare to go with a big one.

All that evening we were towing cars and lorries off the Show ground. Grateful drivers giving money to Da for towing. Mostly five shillings. A few gave pound notes and one man, with a Bentley, gave a note for five pounds! Big as a hanky. Black-printed 'THE BANK OF ENGLAND'. The first one I had seen then.

One well-dressed lady gave Da sixpence.

Dai and Da were soaked, covered in mud and cow muck.

That evening after supper, I heard Da talking: "Made more money in this one day than in a year of farming."

Mam had a new coat. Megan - those red shoes she wanted.

Next year, on Show Day, we all said, "I hope it's sunny." But I knew Da (and Megan) were praying for rain.

-----<>-----

FENCES

April, it was. Daffys in the hedges. 'Lent lilies,' Megan called them.

Heifers, full of spring fever, had pushed the fence down.

Dai helping Da fix it. Me, holding the staples, passing the hammer (and looking for birds' nests).

Up the lane comes Blod Williams - wearing lipstick. 'Tarty' Mam used to call her.

"Afternoon, Mr Price, Dai and Huw-boy."

"Good afternoon, Blodwen," says Da. But not warmly.

Blod smiling at Dai. One of his laces seems to have come undone, suddenlike.

Blodwen walks on, Dai watching after.

Nearly finished the fence, comes a 'calling' across the valley. Blodwen - not singing, not shouting, a sort of yowling. Funny it was. A pulling in my belly, like a magnet, across the valley.

"Vixen calling," says Da, tightening the wire. I pass a staple and the hammer.

>>>

Dai gone, sneaking up the hedgeside.
Da calls, "David."
Must have been further away than I thought. Or gone deaf, suddenlike.
"Diawl," said Da, putting down the hammer. "Dog fox!"
Lighting his pipe then. Puffing, looking dreamy. Like he was remembering something.

Dai missed supper.
In our bedroom, light out, I said, "What happened?"
"Mind yours," said Dai, and I knew he was tapping the side of his nose in the darkness. Tone of his voice said, 'No questions, no answers'.
I lay quiet, wondering.
Home from school next day, me asking where Dai was.
"Your father is taking him round the boundary. Telling him about fencing - to make sure creatures don't get out." Mam winking at Megan.
"Bad fences make bad neighbours."
"More neighbours," says Megan, winking at Mam.
Me not understanding.

I do now, though. Two years on, today, Da took me 'Round the Boundary'.

-----<>-----

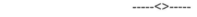

BETTER THAN A PARROT

I read a book called 'Treasure Island'. And I wanted a parrot to sit on my shoulder and say, "Pieces of eight," like the one in the book did.
At the Pet Shop, I was disappointed to learn that a parrot cost a fortune.
Dai said, "Get a jackdaw," and Alan Pritchard told me it would talk, if I split its tongue with a sixpence.
So, with Alan, I climbed the cliff-face of the Darren above Cwm Cadno. Dozens of jackdaws nesting up there in crevices. Their nests, masses of sticks and sheep's wool. Very smelly. >>>

We took a fledgling for training to say, "Pieces of eight," when sitting on my shoulder. I called him 'Jack Daw' and kept him in a box, with wire netting over. Jack Daw would crouch down, beak open, wings shaking, and call, "Jak, jak," when I came to feed him, with egg yolks, bread - milk sodden - and worms from near the muck heap.

I looked at his tongue but couldn't see how to split it with a sixpence. So I didn't. But I didn't need to. He would say, "Jak, jak," which meant "I'm hungry," and "Jak, jak," which meant "It's playtime," and "Jak jak," meaning, "I love you."

Jack Daw got so friendly, he would sit on my shoulder like a parrot. And on the top of my head like a pigeon on a statue. Same problem, sometimes.

In the evenings the wild jackdaws would fly over, on their way back to the Darren. Calling down, "Jak jak."

Jack Daw would get restless, answering and hopping, excited, round his prison. I wondered if he would rather be out there with the others.

But I kept him. **My** Jack Daw!

One day, back from school, I found the cage was empty. Searching, I saw some feathers. Dai said the cat had ate it, but I didn't believe him. Or didn't want to.

I knew that Jack Daw was with the others. Living in a crevice on the Darren.

I saw him flying over every evening, and calling to me, "Jak, jak."

Much better than a parrot.

-----<>-----

COCKLES AND ICECREAM

Our Sunday School teacher was Ceinwen Jenkins. In her thirties - or her forties.

"She'll not marry," said Megan. "Too straightlaced, afraid to let her hair down."

In a bun, it was, black and shiny. 'Did she sleep in it, then?' I wondered.

Every Sunday, Ceinwen Jenkins would cross the valley, with her prayer book, for taking 'school'. Crossing the little plank bridge.

Every Sunday, me and my brothers would put a stone under the bridge end.

>>>

Every Sunday, Ceinwen Jenkins would cross the plank bridge. Never learning. Tipping into the water (only shallow). Black shoes and stockings soaking, treading the pedals of the organ. Singing "Jesus wants me for a sunbeam."

Every August 'Outing' to the sea-side. Can't go, though, till you're eleven.

My first Outing was to Porth-y-Pyscod. Me so excited. Never seen the sea.

Coach was waiting early morning. Mam gave me five shillings for spending. So did Megan.

Children singing, led by Ceinwen, "Jesus wants me" and "Bread of Heaven." Smashing. (Ate all of my sandwiches before we got as far as Brecon)

Lovely at the sea-side, paddling in the water. Eating cockles and icecream.

On the quayside, black baskets for catching lobsters. Smelling of tar and fishes. Eating icecream and cockles.

Fishing boats in the harbour. Their nets spread out and hanging, for drying in the sunshine. Eating cockles and icecream.

Back on the coach now, tired and sunburned.

Coach swaying on the corners. Queasy.

Suddenly - cockles and icecream, icecream and cockles.

Ceinwen Jenkins helping, holding me, wiping my face with her hanky. Lacy, smelling of lavender. I remember so clearly.

Hairpins dropping, her bun undoing. Black hair silky around her shoulders. Looked quite pretty.

"You sit by me, Huw," said Ceinwen, putting her arm around my shoulders.

Sleepy, me. Dozing, head on her bosoms. Smelling lavender and mothballs. Bosoms jerking. Was she crying? Soon I was sleeping.

Every Sunday, my brothers would put a stone under the plank-bridge. Every Sunday, I would go, after, and move it.

No wet shoes and stockings, now, in the chapel.

Ceinwen Jenkins never married. Too straightlaced, afraid to let her hair down.

-----<>-----

When I was little and a cow was 'beasting'. we would take it, on a halter, to the bull at Morgan's.

Da and Morgan would stand talking about prices at the market and I would sit on the gate watching. The cow standing impassive while the bull mounted. A bit of snorting and mooing, then it was over. But it all seemed so natural.

A few years later we had 'Artificial Insemination'. Da called it 'The New Way'.

"We can have the best bulls in the country."

When a cow was ready, I would take tuppence, run down the meadow to the phone box on the Main Road. There I would ask the girl on the switchboard for Usk Three-One.

"Please send Lavenham Undaunted to Price, Cwm Cadno."

A man would come then, wearing a white coat, in a van, with a syringe, and Lavenham Undaunted in a test tube. Do strange things in the cow-shed.

I must say the calves were better. Even though the bull calves went straight to market, the heifers were splendid milkers. So the New Way *must* be better.

About this time, Evan Lewis was courting our Megan. Talk of weddings, bridesmaids and dresses.

I wondered if, when the time came for babies, they would still do the same things that people used to, or would it be 'The New Way?'

Half of me hoped it was the old way, but if not, I looked forward to Megan (Mrs Lewis) giving me tuppence for the phone box.

I would run down the meadow. Ask the girl to get me Usk Three-One. But I wouldn't say, "Lavenham Undaunted."

I would ask them to send the man, in his white coat, with his syringe and a test tube - and Johnny Weismuller!

-----<>-----

WITTY BITS

In a cottage at the top-end of Cwm Cadno lived Mrs Evans. An old lady in her eighties. She lived on her own then with a few chickens. "My chukies," she used to call them.

On Tuesdays, Mrs Evans would go to market. After, I would carry her basket, full of shopping, from the bus-stop up to her cottage.

She called me "Huwboy." I think she liked me.

All her children and grand-children lived in New Zealand. She never saw them. But they would write to her at Christmas. Sometimes.

Then she would show me the letters and ask me to read them. Often.

We would sit there by her fire, in the lamplight, and I would read to her about kiwis and tree-ferns, sheep and horses, weddings and christenings, hot springs and Maoris.

Mrs Evans would sit there, holding a hanky, sniffing sometimes.

Now and then she would give me presents - a cup that Mr Evans had won with his sheep dog. One Christmas, a box with dates in. She had taken all the stones out and put marzipan into the middles. "These are for you, Huwboy."

After market one day, Mrs Evans gave me a booklet, 'Witty Bits'.
It had cost fourpence when she had bought it in 1930.

The pages were brown and faded, but it was filled with clever sayings, jokes and word puns. I loved it.

Learned them in dozens, and told them to my friends and my relations. Not everybody thought them funny. Some of the puns were real 'groaners' and my friends would throw things at me, when I used them. But I liked that.

Later, I learned how to slip them into the conversation, spontaneous-like. Made me realise how rich and subtle is language .

Since then, words delight me. I like playing with the meanings. Even writing little stories about when I lived in Cwm Cadno.

Mrs Evans died soon after. Now, whenever I tell a story or slip a 'groaner' into the conversation, I remember Mrs Evans and her kindness to 'Huwboy'.

-----<>-----

It was a hot day, and I mean HOT. We don't get many in Wales.

My Four-Ten shotgun, new, light as it was, seemed heavy. Lovely, though. Stock polished, dark red mahogany. The barrel - a kind of dark blue, sort of grape colour. It was a present, now I was thirteen. Made me feel a Man.

Nothing to shoot at, too hot. Rabbits underground. Squirrels hiding in topmost branches. Pigeons somewhere else. Suddenly lonely. Unusual for me, like being on my own, mostly.

Over the bridge, movement. Someone is coming.

Rhiannon from Trehelig. Bit older than me, her. Pretty she looks. Blue skirt, white blouse, with flowers, Swiss-like. Beginning to fill it too. Mysterious this, to boys.

"Hello, Rhiannon."

"Hello, Huw. Shooting?"

"Squirrels, shilling a tail. Tree rats, Da calls them."

"Hot today."

"Very."

Then me, greatly daring, "Fancy a walk, then?"

"Where to?"

"Up by the stream."

Rhiannon nodded shyly.

Gun hidden under the bridge, we walk by the water, sheep paths through bracken.

Each bend a dipper, rising, skimming ahead and piping, "Intruders." (Nesting under the bridge, thinks I don't know that.)

By the old sheep pen, now just boulders covered in lichen, Rhiannon stops.

"I fancy a paddle."

Shoes off, sitting on the bank, splashing and giggling. Water so shallow.

"Let's make a dam," I said, not expecting a girl to want to.

Barefoot and lovely, skirt tucked in knicker-legs, Rhiannon wades in. Passes me stones and handfuls of moss. Water rising slowly.

Above our knees now, cold from springs deep in the mountain.

"Be able to swim soon," said Rhiannon, looking at me from under her lashes.

Fool as I was, I said, "No costume, no towel."

"Who's looking?" said Rhiannon, smiling sweet-like. >>>

I remembered a picture, 'Aphrodite Rising from the Waves.' I wondered - would she?

"I will if you will," I said, heart thumping.

"All right - but you first," she said, still smiling.

Not wearing much anyway that day. Soon off, and me in the water. Cold but lovely.

"Come on then," I called.

"In a minute. Look at that Polly Wagtail."

It was perched on a boulder, bobbing and curtseying, like we were royal.

I splashed about, pretending to be swimming, waiting. Rhiannon sat there, watching.

"Come on then," I called.

"Changed my mind now," she said, looking at the wagtail forwards but watching me sideways.

Silly I felt then, splashing to show I didn't care.

Chilling now, in the water. Got to come out sometime; might as well be now.

Standing up, feet numb, I stumble on stones, climb out, not looking at Rhiannon but knowing she is watching me. I dressed, still wet.

"You promised," I said, disappointed. She still looked lovely.

"I was lying then," she said.

'Truthful, at least,' I thought. 'A truthful liar.'

I smiled at that and the sun seemed warm again.

Rhiannon leading, we walked through the bracken down to where the bridge was.

Not smiling now, she said, "I'm sorry, Huw. I had to, no brothers, see." That smile again.

Under the bridge to get the gun. Back up, she's gone.

Rhiannon's married now. Mrs Dai Parry. Three children.

I see her sometimes in the market. She smiles then and looks at me sideways.

I like that.

Aphrodite.

A walker, crossing Bryn Cadno, had dropped a match or cigarette-end into the heather.

There were fire engines, as bright as cherries, on the hill tracks.

Sweating firemen in thick blue jackets and yellow helmets, whacking at the flames with rubber beaters.

I knew where the skylarks were nesting, but could do nothing to help them.

After - just desolation. Acres of heather and whinberries burned to a cinder. The limestone boulders, once mellow with lichen, were white as sheep's skulls on the mountain. From a distance, it looked like snowfall, even in Summer. Would it ever recover?

Da said, "Nature abhors a vacuum."

A year later, I walked over Bryn Cadno.

Black ashes, white boulders, stark in the sunshine. But I found a birch tree, tiny, growing from a seed blown there during the winter. Alone in the starkness.

Next year, on the boulders, spots of orange - lichens returning. Between the boulders, fleshy green things, like wet rubber. No birch tree - a sheep had found it.

In the third year, brilliant green mosses covered the blackness. The lichens, growing strongly, softened the outlines of the boulders. In places, patches of grass grew, and at the edges of the burnt part, heather and whinberry expanding, competing with the mosses.

Each year - greener. The boulders - softer.

Now, when I walk over Bryn Cadno, only I know how it once was. I hear the skylarks and remember Da saying, "Nature abhors a vacuum."

-----<>-----

MIXED POSIES 16

In Cwm Cadno, the old houses on the hillside were ruins, long deserted.

Just stone walls covered in mosses and lichen. Fireplaces empty. Ivy on the chimneys, rooms full of nettles. No-one remembered who lived there.

But every springtime the gardens were full of flowers. Snowdrops, primroses and daffys. Sometimes a lily.

In one old garden, a rose grew, defiant.

Mam and Megan would pick the flowers for market. In bunches of a dozen. (Flowers come in tens now - decimalisation!"

Mam made something special for the Market. "Mixed Posies," she called them.

Different flowers from the gardens, and the meadows, depending on the season.

Each posy, a mass of colour, fragrant from violets, budding roses or stocks, sweet scented.

Only sixpence for a posy. Townsfolk loved them.

Mam is gone now. But sometimes in the Market I remember "Mixed Posies" - and Mam.

-----<>-----

Sometimes, just lately, I go back to Cwm Cadno. My wife, Mary, says I shouldn't. She knows how much it hurts me. But I have to.

I stand up by the Darren and look down into Cwm Cadno.

Most of the trees sold for timber. The hedges, with foxgloves and daffys 'grubbed out'. This being 'more efficient'.

The old stone buildings replaced by concrete and asbestos.

The orchard and Mam's garden, vanished.

No duck-pond or bee-hives.

The lane tarmac'ed. Lineposts crossing the meadow.

I think, 'One day, if I made a fortune, I would buy back Cwm Cadno from the strangers'.

Replant the orchard and the beech trees, put back the hedges - the foxgloves and daffys - and the Garden.

Replace the concrete with mellow buildings. Pennywort and harts-tongue growing in the mortar.

Dig a new duck-pond and make Cwm Cadno like it once was.

And I stand there, a damned fool, crying for the magic of my childhood.

I turn and walk away, then, over the unchanged mountain. The buzzards are still circling, the skylarks are still singing and the curlews are still calling, as they used to.

Even the raven in the thorn tree, hoarsely croaking my reappearance, is saying I must never go back to Cwm Cadno.

And I won't

Until the next time.

-----<>-----

Poems based on Cwm Cadno experiences will be found in 'A Curlew's Cry'.

MICHAEL TOD

Michael Tod was born in Dorset and lived near Weymouth until his family moved to a hill farm in Wales when he was eleven. His childhood experiences on the Dorset coast and in the Welsh mountains have given him a deep love and knowledge of wild creatures and the countryside, which is reflected in many of these poems, kernels and stories, and in his 'Squirrel' novels.

Married, with three children and three grandchildren, he still lives, works and walks in his beloved Welsh hills, but visits his old haunts in Dorset whenever he can.

Michael Tod claims to be a founder member of the Ninety-one Campaign for Readable and Accessible Poetry (N.O.C.R.A.P.)